PYTHON FOR INTERMEDIATE

A practical guide for intermediate using of Python

Will Norton

Text Copyright © [Matthew]

Legal & Disclaimer

Table of Contents

Introduction

Machine learning is one of the most fast-developing computer technologies in this decade and is estimated to occupy the mainstream industry by 2025.

A lot of industries are developing applications and algorithms to use machine learning functionalities. For example, Google is developing a machine-learning algorithm to verify the search results quality.

We can implement machine learning functionalities using different languages such as Python, R, and Java.

However, Python is said to give excellent results from the data scientist's perspective. In the previous book of this module, we have discussed Python programming language. This book explains advanced Python concepts from a data scientist perspective.

A lot of the topics we will discuss will give a clear understanding of its importance in the machine learning environment.

Why we wrote this book?

There are fewer resources that provide valuable knowledge related to Python that is required for improving machine learning skills.

We wrote a book that can help beginners to grasp the complex python topics to use them in implementing machine learning algorithms.

Python has a lot of third-party libraries that can help a data scientist to improve his technical ability.

However, to use these third-party libraries it is essential to master advanced Python programming. For this sole reason, we have written a book that lets you understand various Python topics easily.

How to use this book?

This book is a comprehensive guide to Python and also comprises various programming examples.

We recommend you to install Python in your system and work with the Python code to look at the results. Dealing with errors all by yourselves will help you understand the essence of the programming language.

There are a lot of books that can help you master the Python programming, but there are only a few books that will help you think like a programmer.

This book is one of them. All the best and have a happy learning experience. Let us go!

Chapter 1: What is Python? Why Python?

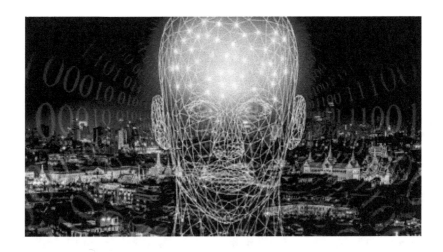

Python is a programming language that has been declared as one of the easiest programming languages to learn for beginners.

Apart from its simple syntax and intuitive functionalities, the availability of abundant resources is also a reason for Python's success among the masses.

Python is the most popular language in GitHub and comprises thousands of open source projects and third-party libraries that can help you create complex software.

Python is also a recommended language to learn for enthusiastic data scientists.

Machine learning, a famous computer science branch relies on Python libraries to analyze the data. In this book, we will look at Python functionalities from a machine learning perspective. In the next section, we will discuss Python functionalities with good, valid technical information.

Why Python is famous?

There are over 100 programming languages available for computer programmers and computer scientists nowadays. Out of all, Python has occupied a prominent position because of its active community which is always trying to clear off the bugs and update with new features.

A study proposed why Python is famous among programmers. We will in this section discuss some of those reasons that made Python a programmer's favorite.

Here are the valid reasons:

1) Quality

When you create programs with Python, they are often of high quality. The users encounter fewer bugs and it is easy to update the programs using different Python modules.

Python supports various programming paradigms such as procedural and object-oriented programming to reuse the code effectively. It is also easily readable because of indentation techniques. This high quality in the programming syntax had made programmers fell in love with it.

2) Productivity

Other programming languages such as Java and C are statistically typed languages and require a huge amount of code to even process very fewer data.

Python simplifies the code to be written and requires only half of the programming code when compared to the other languages. This increases productivity and can adversely increase the quality of applications that are being developed.

3) Portability

Unlike Java, which runs its applications only when a JVM is present Python can run software applications on any platform. All you need to do is to add a few lines of code that will process the software to run on other platforms.

Python applications can also be deployed to run in web and database environments with a slight change in code. All these portable advantages make developers use Python as a primary language when developing cross-platform applications.

4) Third-party Libraries

Python has a lot of default functions in the standard library. There are mathematical and statistical functions that can be used in developing data science applications.

However, standard library functions are often not sufficient to develop complex software. Here comes the concept of third-party libraries which can be easily imported to a Python project. With the help of third-party libraries, you can develop complex and advanced software using Python.

5) Enjoyment

As simple and intuitive it is, Python's success also depends on its level of enjoyment to the developers. It is easy to maintain and comprises fewer hiccups than the other programming languages. Python has various modules that can automate tasks. All these advantages bind up to make Python an entertaining programming language for the developers.

Because of the above technical reasons, Python has become famous among the programming community and has expanded its user base. In the next section, we will describe some Python applications in day-to-day life.

Applications of Python

Python is used by approximately 1.5 million developers according to the statistics. A lot of websites, APIs, software are developed using Python as a primary language.

This success of Python is also because of its open-source nature that lets programmers use the language as they like. This is the reason why Python is also used as a scripting language by many hackers.

However, it is not evident to call Python as a scripting language on this remark. We consider Python as a multi-use language that can be useful for many fields and users.

Here are some multi-national companies that use Python for their products:

a) Google extensively uses Python to build and update its search engine crawlers.

b) YouTube was initially written on Python. A lot of YouTube integration services still use Python.

c) A lot of Netflix recommendation algorithms use Python to resource them effectively.

d) Dropbox, a famous storage service uses Python to encrypt the files.

Apart from these few examples, Python is also used in iRobot to develop Robots.

Here are some technical fields where Python is extensively used:

a) Systems programming

This is a branch of computer science where we can develop system management tools such as compilers, interpreters and shell tools that can interact with the system at the kernel level. Python is very adaptable to this branch of computer science as it has several extensible libraries that can help to create effective programs.

b) Internet

Python is an easy language to create small internet scripts. A lot of script kiddies use programs developed using Python to crack account passwords. A lot of brute forcing tools also use Python to automate dictionary attacks on an authenticated server.

Python is also famous for developing web applications that can store sensitive information. A lot of WebCrawler and web analysis services use Python to curate the information.

c) Integration systems

A lot of hardware components such as Arduino works effectively only when they are programmed to do. Usually, embedded systems work well with traditional structural languages such as C and C++.

Python has a lot of libraries that can help to integrate already written python code to embedded systems.

d) Database programming

Databases are an essential entity to store and manipulate information. There are a lot of database query languages to store and query data. However, Python is used by many database administrators to constantly monitor the intrusion detection system that is available.

There are a lot of Python libraries that can help developers to automatically check for viruses and store a backup in the remote server.

e) Machine Learning

Machine learning is a booming computer science field where we can analyze the information and data that is present. Python has a lot of libraries such as SciPy and Pandas to maintain the data in a significant way.

This book will list out various Python features to become good at machine learning.

Apart from these fields, Python is also used by hackers, malware reverse engineers, and Computer scientists to do various analytic experiments.

In the next section, we will discuss the advantage of Python over various other languages that are available.

Let us go!

What are Python's strengths?

Python is suggested for beginners by experienced programmers because it helps you to understand all the basics that every programming language use.

Python is usually a combined mixup of all the programming paradigms that are used. We will give you a clear understanding of this below.

a) *Supports both functional and object-oriented*

Python, unlike Java and C++, uses functional programming along with the object-oriented paradigm. This gives a scope to learn both technologies as a beginner.

A lot of core concepts such as polymorphism, inheritance, and functions will be covered while learning Python.

b) Open-source

Python is developed by enthusiast contributors from all around the world. It is free to create programs and distribute them.

This open-source nature gives programmers to experiment with the code and create some innovative applications.

c) Powerful

It is powerful when compared with other popular programming languages. It supports dynamic typing and is unnecessary to declare the variable and list sizes before compiling the program.

Python uses a garbage mechanism and sends all the useless system variables to dump. This improves the performance of the program in an exponential manner.

d) Default tools

Python offers a lot of very useful system tools. It can perform a lot of string operations easily using these default tools. It is also important to understand these modules to perform operations in a better way using Python.

e) Easy to use

Unlike traditional programming languages such as C and C++ Python is easy to use. C and C++ offer different paradigms that can confuse developers to operate. Python uses less indentation and it is easy to maintain the code. Python also is better than Java because it is not a statically typed language. In java, you need to introduce different useless variables to maintain the flow of the program structure. However, in Python, you use only what you need. This is one of the reasons Python is considered a better language for developing Machine Learning applications.

How to learn Python?

Python has a generous community that shares a lot of resources and sample projects to encourage beginners to understand the importance and beauty of Python.

This book is also a genuine approach to help you understand all the moderate level topics of Python to implement in developing Artificial intelligence and data science applications.

We suggest you to look at an open-source project and understand the essence of the logic by the constant implementation of the topics you have learned in this book.

That's it.

In this chapter, we have got a thorough introduction to the importance of Python from various sections.

Hope this chapter gave you a sufficient introduction to help you get hooked up with the topic. I

n the next chapter of this book, we will discuss different ways to install Python in the system.

Let us go!

Chapter 2: How to install python on your PC?

In the previous chapter, we have discussed the importance of Python along with its important features. In this chapter, we will discuss installing

Python in various operating systems. We will also discuss installing third party modules in Python using various package managers.

Let us start!

Checking Python Version

Usually, in Linux and Mac ox operating systems, Python is installed by default. However, it is recommended to check the version of Python using the command prompt.

Windows users need to download the installation package from the Python website.

How to check the Python version?

Open terminal or command prompt depending on your system to check whether Python is installed.

Always try to open the terminal using the administrator privileges for accurate results.

Enter the following formats:

python

python 2

python 3

If Python is installed on the system, you will get a result that displays the version of the Python that is installed.

It will also provide various options that can be very useful for beginners to understand popular commands for managing Python programs.

However, if there are no traces of the Python installation folder in the system then the terminal will return an error. Please check with the above commands in your operating system, and if your terminal sends a command error, then it is time to install the Python using the below guide.

Follow along!

How to install Python in windows?

Step 1:

First, it is important to choose the version you are willing to install in your system. We recommend you to look at the next chapter to understand about different available Python versions.

You can also look at Python online documentation to choose the suitable python version according to your requirements.

Step 2:

After selecting the python version, visit the official website to download the Python version. You need to select a 32 or 64-bit option to download the version that will be installed with no errors.

You can either download a .msi package or a .exe application according to your wish. After downloading the installation file, all you need to do is open the file with administrator privileges.

Step 3:

After we start the installation, you will get an interface that asks to enter the directory to install Python.

You can either install Python with the default directory or can change the directory according to your requirements.

Note: Make sure that there are no spaces in the directory names as sometimes Python installation will give an error.

Step 4:

At the last step of the installation, you need to update the environment variable so that Python will run on the command prompt on the system. Once the installation is finished you can crosscheck whether the installation is successful using the procedure explained before.

With this, we have learned about installing a basic Python package in the system.

In the next section, we will discuss various Python modules necessary for developing complex Python programs.

What are the other alternatives?

Python users should remember that there are several replica interpreters of Python that can be installed on the windows system.

Some are CPython, Pypy which are famous for their customization abilities.

However, we recommend you to try the original Python versions for advanced usage abilities and faster processing.

How to install Python in Mac OS?

Mac operating system has a default Python 2.x version already installed on the Python operating system. Mac operating system uses Python to control various system operations.

However, if you are keen on updating your Python version for developing programs follow the below section.

Step 1:

In the first step, you need to visit the Python official download page. The website will automatically determine your system configuration and will list you a .dmg package installer to download.

Thoroughly check the version name before you are downloading.

Step 2:

After clicking on the .dmg package installer you will be asked to enter your operating system authentication detail for security reasons.

The installer will also ask you about the default directory location.

Step 3:

In the next step, you need to enter the customization options. You can also use the automatic option to let the installer give the best results according to your system configuration. After it finishes the installation it is recommended to reboot the system and check the Python version using the terminal as mentioned in the previous sections.

Are you not interested in the Terminal operation?

Usually, Python programs are compiled in the command line interpreter or terminal. Normally, Programmers need to save a python script using a text editor and compile it from the terminal.

However, a lot of the developers are not comfortable dealing with command-line operations.

For programmers who are more inclined towards graphical user interfaces, Python provides a GUI package to install on the system.

This package is known as the Tkinter application and can be downloaded from the Python official website.

After installing can also add add-ons to customize your graphical interface.

Installing/Upgrading Python in Linux

Linux is an operating system that is used by most of the programmers and technical enthusiasts to perform tasks and to develop programs. Linux, unlike Windows and Mac, relies mostly on command line operations.

Usually, python is pre-installed in a lot of Linux distros.

If you are unaware, you can just check the Python version and proceed with the further installation process as given below.

Step 1:

You can download the Python .deb package from the Python's official website. You can use sudo operations to install the package in your system.

If you are not technically sound enough to install using the sudo operation, you can also use package managers such as RPM to install the python package.

Step 2:

After installing the package all you need to do is enter python on the terminal and look for the obtained results. You can also upgrade Python to the newer versions by changing the build script present in the Python installation folder.

In Linux, you may face conflicts while using two different versions of Python in the same system.

So, always make sure you have uninstalled the previous Python versions from the system.

Using REPL

REPL is the most basic Python component necessary to run arithmetic operations.

This component is responsible to input the values and output results. It is like a lexical analysis tool for Python. You can use REPL mode to check whether or not python is installed.

Here are some operations you can perform to confirm the Python installation in the system:

a) Do arithmetic operations

Run the following commands on your command line:

>>> 4747+3737

>>> 3424*242

>>> 63634/27

If you are getting results with no errors, then Python is successfully installed in the system.

b) Assigning variables

Variables are an entity that can store values and repeat them whenever we need it.

Here is an example:

>>> r = 446

Now try to print the assigned variable

>>> r

If you get 446 as the result then you can confirm that Python is successfully installed in your system.

Learning about Help command

Python provides a help command that will inform you about various operations that the interpreter can perform.

You can also check the online documentation to know more about the system functions and libraries.

Here is the format:

>>> help

By using this command, you can print out all the function prompts in order. Help () function can understand details about different system functions.

Every IDE also comprises a help folder that can be used to regulate information.

Using pip

Python is a programming language that uses modules and packages to develop an efficient program.

A lot of modules need to be downloaded from websites such as GitHub into the system.

To make this procedure easy, Python has developed a PyPI index that lists out all the eligible python modules.

Learning how to use pip is an essential skill for programmers. Pip can be installed using the Sudo commands.

Before trying to install a module using pip, we suggest you look at the Python module index.

After you enter the module name, the pip search module will start batch searching the module from different resources. If it finds the module, then using the downloading module it will install on your preferred directory.

Here is the command:

sudo pip install {enter the package name here}

Pip can be used in all the operating systems available.

All you need to have is a supported Python version in the system.

Using easy_install

easy_install is another alternative to pip to install different modules directly into the system.

With easy_install you can directly change the setup script to automatically make changes to the package being downloaded.

However, unlike pip, it is not simple and needs advanced learning capabilities to master it.

We recommend you to look at easy_install documentation to learn more about it.

Other IDE's to download

In this chapter, we discussed the default Python interpreter that Python comes with.

It is often recommended for beginners to make things look simpler instead of confusing them with different functionalities.

However, if you are interested, you can check out different IDE's that can develop Python programs.

We recommend Pycharm IDE to understand the different complex functionalities of Python.

Pycharm IDE also offers various debugging features to make the development of programs easy.

How to run a Python script?

After installing every necessary component, it is now time to know how to run a python script in the command line environment.

Step 1:

First, open a text editor of your choice and create a file with extension .py. In this text file enter the script and save it in your desired folder.

Step 2:

Now start the Python interpreter using Python command in the terminal. After entering the Python instance, you need to enter the following command to run the program.

>>> python filename.py

If there are no errors in the program, your file will run according to your requirements.

However, if there are any runtime errors and warning your program will be halted and it will display the results.

With this, we have completed a brief introduction to installing Python in different operating systems.

It is important to use this chapter as a reference to install different modules that will be introduced in the next chapters in this book.

In the next chapter, we will discuss different Python versions. As said before, it is important to choose the best version according to your needs.

Let us go!

Chapter 3: Different Versions of Python?

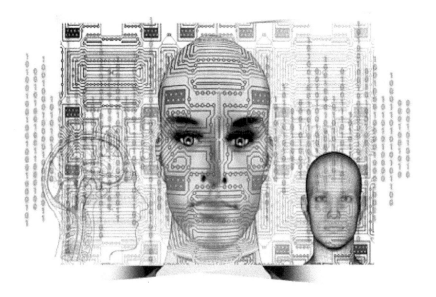

Python is a programming language that has been constantly developed by various programmers individually by collaborating with different resources.

In 1984, python's first version was released and for years it has been constantly updated with various functionalities.

In this chapter, we will discuss various Python versions and their abilities.

Let us go!

Which version most programmers use?

As of this writing, Python programmers largely rely upon Python 2.x versions for developing applications. Even after 10 years of their release, Python 3.x versions are not widely used by the community for its complex implementation of the functions.

However, Python 3.x versions also provide a lot of new features for advanced machine learning applications.

As this book focuses on Machine learning, we recommend you to try Python 3.x versions to develop applications.

Why are versions important?

When a programming language is developed there is often scope for bugs and security issues that can destroy the reputation.

This is one reason programming languages are often updated to newer versions with better compatibility.

Python developers in 2008 have started providing a 3.x version of Python with advanced functionalities, but with a change in syntax and implementation format.

Programmers are already comfortable with the 2.x version functionalities and did not go along with the flow.

However, as years passed Python 3.x has improved drastically and is now an efficient version of Python with advanced features.

The Python downloads homepage provides all these versions to download at a click.

All you need to do is understand and analyze which software version fits your needs. In the next section, we will provide complete features of all the major Python versions that got released.

Let us go!

History of Python versions

a) Python version 1

The first version of Python is developed and released in 1984. At that time, C is a popular language and is holding a good percentage of the programming market. By 1995, the python developers have included higher-order functions such as lambda and maps in the package.

The first version of Python is a huge success when looked at from a programming perspective. However, it is still not a programmer's favorite due to different compatibility reasons.

b) Python version 2

Python version 2 has changed the impact of Python in the programming world. A lot of new features such as list comprehensions and functional programming are introduced in this version of Python. Also, version 2 has made python function declaration much easier.

A lot of new concepts such as garbage mechanism and operator overloading are introduced to make this version easier to operate and maintain.

Till 2020, Python developers will maintain the version 2 python.

c) Python version 3

Python version 3 didn't do well in the programming arena when it is first introduced. A lot of programmers complained about the function declarations when it is first released.

However, as time passed with updated versions Python has shown its impact in the programming world.

A lot of advanced scientific applications started to use system functions introduced in Python 3 to implement their programs.

Python 3 also made a lot of changes to type declarations and has moved on to become one of the most successful versions of Python.

Which Python version you should choose?

It is a programmer choice to pick up the version he is more comfortable with. However, here is a suggestion that experienced programmers give to the beginners.

" Always chose the version of the Python according to your requirements.

If you want to develop a simple crawler application then it makes sense to use an older version.

If you are trying to build an advanced application that involves various new functionalities, we recommend you to try the newer versions"

Which version is best for Data scientists?

In this book, we mostly discuss Python version 3. This version is more supportive of machine learning libraries and consists of a lot of list operations.

As we deal with a huge chunk of data manipulating list items is a mandatory task. So, we recommend you to try Python version 3 to develop machine learning projects.

Which version is the most popular?

As of now, a lot of web and mobile applications are being developed using Python version 2. However, after 2020 Python will officially stop supporting Python 2 and evidentially after that, we will see a bounce in the number of programmers using Python 3.

According to a recent study conducted by Harvard University, Python 2 is one of the simplest and intuitive Python versions that ever got released.

With this, we have completed a brief introduction to Python versions in this chapter.

In the next chapter, we will discuss functional programming in detail.

Follow along!

Chapter 4: Functional Programming and Comprehension

Functions are a mathematical concept that can be used to repeat the tasks in a definite manner.

Traditional programming languages adopted this in programming to automate repetitive tasks.

However, with time developers started deploying various system functions to make programming languages more intuitive and operative.

In this chapter, we will in detail discuss various functionalities that functional programming offers with a lot of examples.

Follow along!

Characteristics of Functional programming

Functional programming contrary to the belief can cooperate with both imperative and object-oriented paradigms.

Here are some of the objectives to remember to reconsider whether a programming language supports a complete functional paradigm or not.

1) Functions are also objects. They can be used to perform every single task that objects can perform. They can be used to call a function from within a function.

2) A lot of functional programming paradigms use recursions to loop the structures. Some functional programming paradigms only offer recursion for looping the tasks.

3) Functional programming also works with lists. They are often used to process and loop through the lists.

4) Functional programming is not very comfortable in dealing with statements. However, they can be used very effectively to evaluate the expressions that hold a logical entity.

5) Functional programming also offers higher-order functions with exact precision.

Python follows all the characteristics mentioned above and is called a pure functional language. In the next section, we will in detail discuss using functions in Python.

Let us go!

What are functions?

Functions are a reusable code segment that can be used to repeat the tasks all at a time according to the specified needs.

For example, Look at the following pattern:

' {}'

'{}{}'

'{}{}{}'

For our requirement, we need to display 100 of these pairs in a straight line. You can use the print function to display the result after a lot of hard work.

However, this method is not feasible and is not preferred by programmers.

Here, functions can be used to assign the pattern and call them how many times we need and wherever we need.

You can use a looping statement to loop the pattern 100 times.

In the next section, we will achieve this result using functions in Python.

Follow along!

How to define a function?

The function should be defined according to certain regular specifications that Python language possesses.

Here is the format that functions use in Python

def {Enter name of the function} [Enter the parameters here]

Here is an example:

def sum(a,b)

After defining a function all you need to do is create a step by step logical expression for the body of the function.

How to call a function?

After defining a function, you need to know the procedure to call it whenever you need it.

Function calls can be achieved in Python by using the following format:

Nameofthefunction ()

Exercise 1: Print 100 lines of the '{}' pattern using a function

Here is the Python code:

```
def funpattern()
{
   for (i=100;i++)
   {
      print ( " {}")
      i++;
   }
}
Print( " Here is the result")
funpattern()
```

Function parameters

Parameters are necessary for functions to define default values. Variables are usually pointed out to parameters in the function and are necessary for logical execution.

There are usually default parameters that define the essence of the function.

Here is the format:

[Function parameter 1, Function parameter 2 ...... Function parameter n]

It is important to remember that the function parameter can be a dynamic number.

You can usually use these parameters to return values. In the next section, we will give an example that will help you understand recursion in detail.

Follow along!

What is recursion?

Recursion is a mathematical phenomenon where a function calls itself until the condition is satisfied. Recursion can decrease the code length of the program very effectively.

A lot of programmers determine recursive functions as an easy way to achieve complete performance from the program.

Here is an example:

```
def result(example):
    if example == 0: return 0
    elif example == 1: return 1
    else: return result(example-1)+result(example-2)
```

Explanation of the program:

In the above program, we use a recursive function to find the Fibonacci numbers according to your input.

Here is a list of steps that we followed:

1) First of all, we created a function using the def reserved keyword and the function name along with a parameter.

2) This function uses a single parameter 'example' that is used to represent the number of Fibonacci numbers that need to be generated in the sequence.

3) In the next step, we created a control flow conditional statement that checks whether a number satisfies the Fibonacci sequence or not.

4) In the conditional statement, the result is always returned using the function.

5) In the next step, we use recursive mechanism to repeat the function logic and print the results.

6) The last step in the function informs to end the recursive function after it satisfies the parameter.

This is how the python uses functional programming to generate results. Python also supports higher-order functions such as Lambda for advanced operations.

How functional programming is essential for Machine Learning?

It is mandatory to learn functional modules in Python because a lot of third-party machine learning supportive libraries such as Pandas use functions to generate algorithms and graphs.

If you are not aware of defining custom functions it will become troublesome to generate unsupervised and supervised algorithms for a dataset.

Also, it is easy to articulate your logical thoughts into programming using functions. To improve your knowledge of function modules we suggest you read the documentation of various third-party libraries.

Higher-order functions

Python supports higher-order functions. Version 3 provides a lot of higher-order functions such as Lambda, filter, reduce.

This section will describe a lot of these in detail.

Follow along!

What is a higher-order function?

This works in the same way as a recursion. In higher-order functions, parameters are also functions.

You can use n number of functions as parameters and can obtain a function as a result.

Higher-order functions use the iterable concept to analyze different types of functions.

Python provides map() and reduce() functions by default. However, all other higher-order functions should be manually imported to make them work.

A lot of data science applications use higher-order functions to get perfect results.

a) Map

A map is a Python high order function that can be used to transform the position of the data set. In machine learning, the transformation of data points is a common phenomenon and is essential for developing regression algorithms.

Here is the format:

map (Enter the coordinates of data set here, Iteration points)

b) Filter

A filter is a Python higher-order function that can be used to predict the data points according to the scenarios given. This higher-order function is largely used in prediction algorithms.

A lot of video streaming websites such as YouTube and Netflix use filter to store user information to recommend the likewise videos.

Here is the format:

filter (Prediction analysis, Iteration)

3) Compose

Compose is a python higher-order function that can in a significant order input functions as parameters.

It can even use loops as a control flow statement to maintain the logical flow of the program. Compose is often used in advanced data analytics applications.

Here is the format:

compose(Enter the higher-order function here)

{

    // Enter the logical statements here

}

Note:

     Higher-order functions can use the same operating module operations as the remaining programming components.

4) Decorators

Higher-order functions are usually arranged syntactically as function parameters. However, decorators are used to syntactically used to arrange higher-order functions such as lambda functions in correct sequential order.

Decorators can take higher-order functions as arguments and output the instances.

Here is the format:

Decorator(Enter higher-order function 1, Enter higher-order function 2)

Decorators can also be used to implement coroutines and develop complex applications that can take coroutines as function arguments.

Decorators can also be very handy while dealing with any debugging and run-time errors.

To develop machine learning applications, it is always recommended to learn in-depth about different higher-order functions and the parameters they can regulate expressions with.

You can look at Python documentation to know about the different types of higher-order functions that are available.

With this, we have completed a brief introduction to functional programming in Python.

In the next chapter, we will discuss the operator module in detail.

Let us go!

Chapter 5: Operator module in Python

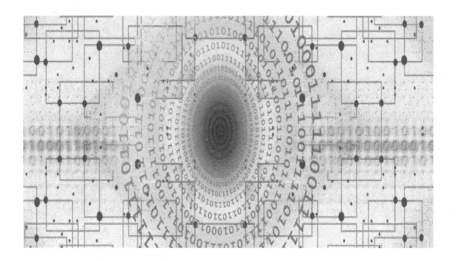

Operators are a mathematical entity which are usually used to combine expressions and statements. In regular mathematical expressions, operators can change the result that is going to obtain.

Python also provides an operator module that can explicitly impact the results that will be obtained. In this chapter, we will in detail discuss various operators that are available in the latest versions of Python.

Follow along!

Mathematical operators

Whenever we are learning a programming language it is essential to master mathematical operators because a lot of programs use mathematical calculations to perform the operations.

For example, to rotate an image in a photo viewer software programmers use transpose of mathematical matrices.

As we all know that mathematics has standard operations known as addition, subtraction, multiplication, and division. Python also provides a modulus operator to obtain the remainder of the mathematical operation.

In the next section, we will explain these mathematical operations with various examples.

Let us go!

```python
# Python code for Addition operator '+'
first = 2
second = 3
result = first+second
# Result will output 5
# Python code for Substraction operator '-'
first = 3
second = 2
result = first-second
# Result will output 1
# Python code for Multiplication operator '*'
first = 2
second = 3
result = first*second
```

```
# Result will output 6
# Python code for Division operator '/'
first = 6
second = 2
result = first/second
# Result will output 3
# Python code for Modulus operator '%'
first = 7
second = 6
result = first%second
# Result will output 1
```

Apart from these basic mathematical operations Python also provides an exponential operator ' * * '. We will give an example for your better understanding.

```
# Python code for Exponential operator '* *'
first = 5
second = 3
result = first * * second
# Result will output 125
```

Note: Python follows hierarchal rules to perform mathematical operations. Python also provides operator precedence to maintain a structural organization for the operations.

This is the sole reason why you need to use parenthesis to categorically group the operators.

Operator precedence

Operator precedence is an essential concept in programming languages while dealing with complex logical expressions. Python gives the exponential operator the highest precedence following by the multiplication, division and modulus operators.

Addition and Subtraction belong to the bottom layer of the operator precedence.

In the next section, we will in-depth explain about the comparison operators that are often used for determining a logic in an expression.

While dealing with complex machine learning data the machine needs to categorize and determine the data using these simple comparison operators. Follow along to know more about it.

Comparison Operators

Comparison operators are used in combining statements and to create logical expressions. There are a lot of comparison operators that can help you easily create logics for many mathematical functions.

In the next section, we will in detail discuss various comparison operators. We have four comparison operators. An example program is given to help you understand how comparison operators work.

Follow along!

a) Greater than

Here is an example to help you understand greater than operator:

```python
# Python code for Greater than Operator '>'
first = 5
second = 3
if ( first > second)
print(" This is the greater perspective")
else
print( " This is the lower perspective")
# Result will output the first statement
```

b) Less than

Here is an example to help you understand less than operator:

```python
# Python code for Greater than Operator '<'
first = 5
second = 3
if ( first < second)
print(" This is the lower perspective")
else
print( " This is the greater perspective")
# Result will output the second statement
```

c) Equal to

Here is an example to help you understand Equal to operator:

```python
# Python code for Greater than Operator '=='
```

```
first = 5
second = 3
if ( first == second)
print(" These two are the same")
else
print( " These two are not the same")
# Result will output the second statement
```

d) Not Equal to

Here is an example to help you understand Not Equal to operator:

```
# Python code for Greater than Operator '!='
first = 5
second = 3
if ( first != second)
print(" These two are not the same")
else
print( " These two are same")
# Result will output the first statement
```

With this, we have completed a small introduction to comparison operators. In the next section, we will in detail discuss Logical operators that are important for performing advanced data science operations.

Follow along!

Logical Operators

Logic is an important assignment component while dealing with complex programs. A lot of python programs consist of conditional and loop statements with logical operators.

There are fundamentally three logical operators which we will now discuss in detail in the next section.

a) and

This is a logical operator that can be used when you are looking forward to printing an expression when two statements are satisfied.

It is represented by 'and'.

Here is an example:

```
first = 2
second = 3
third = 5
if ( first ==2 and second==5)
print(" This is right")
else
print(" This is wrong")
```

Now, the program will check whether both first and second have the same values.

As the second variable is not satisfied ' This is wrong' will be displayed as the result.

b) or

This is a logical operator that can be used when you are looking forward to printing an expression when any one of the two statements are satisfied.

It is represented by 'or'.

Here is an example:

```
first = 2
second = 3
third = 5
if ( first ==2 or second==5)
print(" This is right")
else
print(" This is wrong")
```

Now, the program will check whether any one of the first and second have the same values.

As the first variable satisfies the condition ' This is right' will be displayed as the result.

c) not

This acts as a negation operator. That is, it will print when a condition is not satisfied. It is usually represented by 'not.

With this, we have completed a thorough explanation of operators in Python.

In the next chapter, we will start discussing advanced concepts related to iterations and comprehensions.

Let us go!

Chapter 6: Interaction and Generations in Python

In the previous chapters, we have discussed Python programming concepts that help you create basic programs. Functions and operators are fundamentals of python programming.

However, to create basic machine learning projects you need to dwell much deeper into Python. This section of this book involving three chapters will help you learn about interactions, iterations, and generators in detail.

A lot of these concepts are very essential to create effective machine learning models.

Follow along to know more about it.

What are Interactions?

Usually, Python consists of variables that store values in a memory location to use them whenever needed. Interactions are a special entity that helps you to create code that can change one set of variables when the other changes. You can implement interactions in Python using the SciPy library that is available.

Interactions are inspired by form statistics.

What are Comprehensions?

Comprehensions are a Python programming concept that can help you to create listing sequences such as dictionaries and lists effectively. Using comprehensions, you can automatically create a varied range of list values.

Comprehensions are a dynamic way to deal with complex. They use key and value to represent the instances that are produced.

How Interactions can be used in Python?

Python uses interactions and comprehensions to deal with complex listing programs. A lot of open-source software use interactions to develop brute-forcing tools for a faster dictionary attack. However, for the scope of this book, we will discuss the usage of interactions in Machine learning projects in depth in the next section.

Interactions in Machine learning

Interactions can be used instead of approximations to create machine learning algorithms.

You can use interactions to train the machine learning model. You can even try to change different variables to find out the correct interaction point.

Here is a program:

from sklearn

// This is where we need to import the functions from

regression = folds()

cross-validation()

interactions = (Enter the parameters here)

list()

// Create a list

if ()

[

  // create logic here

]

Explanation:

In this program, an interaction is created to give valid data points to the list.

In a machine learning environment, it is important to create an iterating comprehensive list to list out all the logical data points that are present.

You can also look out for different complex list operations to correlate with interactions and create effective machine learning programs.

What are Generations?

Generations are used to deal with higher-order functions automatically. They can argument the functions and can help you to iterate map and hash functions with simple values. Generator expressions are usually used in advanced Python expressions. They can be used with the help of a yield keyword in Python.

What to do next?

After further learning about interactions and comprehensions, we suggest you solve some advanced project scenarios to understand the essence of these concepts concerning machine learning. You can also use interactions to develop cross-validation techniques in Python. A lot of comprehensive machine learning algorithms use interactions to develop scenarios.

With this, we have completed a brief introduction to Interactions and comprehensions in Python. To further improve your skills we suggest you learn iterators and generators in Python and use all of them collaboratively to develop applications.

In the next chapter, we will in detail discuss iterations in Python programming.

Follow along!

Chapter 7: Iteration in Python

In this chapter, we will in detail explain to you iterative statements in Python. A lot of beginners get confused with the distinction between iterations and looping.

Always remember that looping is a branch of iterative statements. We will in detail discuss looping structures in the last chapter of this book. In this chapter, we will take a peek into the iterative statements that python possesses.

Follow along!

What are iterations?

Iterations in layman terms are simply programming objects that support repetition. Iterations can be used in implementing loops in different programming components and structures such as Tuples and dictionaries.

They are usually mistaken with for loop.

However, they represent 'for - in 'loop.

How to create iterations?

Python is a programming language that supports iterations effectively. It uses various higher-order functions to maintain the flow of iterations.

Also, remember that a lot of iterative principles can be achieved only if they follow certain principles.

a) Initialize an iterator

Usually, iterators are initialized with the help of an object. The _iter_ method is used as an initialization mechanism for iterators in Python.

A lot of machine learning models automatically call this method to initialize an iteration factor.

b) Using next in iterators

As explained initially, iterators are complex operations and often require processes that can forward the data.

Next is a function that can pre-process the information with the help of different iterative principles.

We can use for in loop to effectively coordinate the information present in iterators.

If you are not satisfied with the performance of the program, you can use a stopiteration() method to end the operation.

Here is a program:

class name

def iterative

-init-

Enter the parameters

object.c

stopiterative()

You can also use indexes and generators to further improve your iterative performance.

In the next section, we will in detail discuss the usage of iterators for machine learning projects.

Let us go!

How to use iterators for machine learning projects?

With the principle we have learned in the above section you can iteratively update the parameters for machine learning functions. As we already know that iteration is a set of repeated tasks you need to use it to implement real-world practical projects.

First of all, you need to understand the model you are working upon.

Any model that involves decision trees can be used for creating iterative parameters.

However, In Python Gradient descent is used extensively to create iterative algorithms.

You can also use cost functions to implement different models.

Here is an intuition for iterative programs:

1) Use loss functions create definitive iterative functions

2) You can also use parameters to minimize the overfitting problem of machine learning models.

3) You can also use several initialization parameters to increase the effectiveness of the machine learning model

4) Iterations can be further made effective using the local minimum and global minimum values.

All of these functionalities can be implemented using Max and min functions using the Pandas library in python.

In the below section, we give a python program to help you better understand the topic.

Here is the code:

```
import np

pandas iterator

max (Enter the parameters here)

min (Enter the parameters here)

// Use global variance to decrease the machine learning
model effectiveness
```

You can also Use hyperparameters to better understand the iterative capabilities python provides. A lot of cross-validation techniques use iterators during the pre-processing procedure of machine learning.

With this, we have completed a brief introduction to iterators.

In the next chapter, we will in detail discuss generators with a lot of examples.

Follow along!

Chapter 8: Generators in Python

In the previous chapter, we have in detail discussed iteration principles with a couple of examples. In this chapter, we will further move forward and start discussing in detail about generators in Python.

This is a complex topic that is necessary to develop machine learning applications.

We suggest you to learn developing python generators using practical projects.

Follow along!

What are generators?

Generators are a lot similar to functions in Python. The only difference between functions and generators is the latter uses yield keyword to return the values.

So, for a simple trick just remember whenever you see a yield keyword in the Python programming example it is automatically a generator function.

Here is the format:

def {Enter the function name here}

yield

What are the generator objects?

Generator objects are formed when a generator function is created from scratch. They are usually implemented by the method structures that are present in the Python programming syntax.

Always remember that objects are object-oriented systematic structures and can result in mishaps if not coordinated well.

Here is the format:

generator {Enter the statement here}

object = // enter the generator expressions

What are the applications of generators?

Generators are usually used to deal with complex calculations. They can also be used to create iterable functions that are not coordinated well. They can be used to create complex Fibonacci sequences. Generators are extensively used to develop artificial intelligence applications.

A lot of embedded systems also use generators for faster implementation of hardware resources.

In the next section, we will in detail explain generator principles using a Fibonacci sequence example. Follow along!

Here is the code:

```
def fibonacciexam(parameters)

first,second = 3,4

// use generators

yield

x.first()

x.sexond()

// generator expression

yield.fib()

for (to display results)
```

In this example, the following implementation occurs:

1) First of all, you need to create a definition to initiate the procedure of creating a Fibonacci sequence. You can enter your desired values as input to start the procedure.

2) In the next step, you need to start using generators with the help of yield keyword to assign values to these variables.

Here, variables represent the iteration principle that we are going to look at in the next step.

3) Afterward, you need to create objects to represent the generator expression mechanism. You can use these objects to iterate through the variables and create a varied sequence that follows the Fibonacci sequence.

4) In the end, we again use generators to print the results.

With this program, we understood that generators can decrease the resources that need to be taken care of usually.

How generators can be used in machine learning?

Generators are an excellent component principle to train a scientific model. A lot of machine learning projects use a supervised model to perform operations. A supervised learning system hugely depends on preprocessing techniques to display varied results.

To decrease the overfitting problems in machine learning models generators can be used. You can use arrays to implement generators in Python.

In the next section, we will give an example that will help you to understand the advantages of generators in Python.

Here is the python code:

```
// create a list
List-name = ( Enter the values here)
Def machine
obj1 = gen(parameters)
Obj2 = gen.machine
yield
next(obj1)
```

You can use generators to create ranges between the data points. Here yield represents the generator expression. Machine learning is an extensive subject and learning generators will help you create models without any underfitting and overfitting errors.

With this, we have completed a small explanation about the generator.

In the next chapter, we will in detail discuss designing a project.

Follow along!

Chapter 9: How to code in Python?

This chapter is a simple introduction to basic python syntactical structures that can help you to code in Python. Python is a dynamically typed language and requires very fewer code blocks to define the logic.

Python is composed of different programmatically structures and is important to learn about them to write perfect code.

a) comments

Comments are an easy way to give information to the programmer while reading the code. They are usually followed after a # in the program. Comments are not compiled during run-time.

Here is an example:

this is a definition

def add(enter parameters here)

Comments are first developed to organize code structurally. However, with time comments have become an essential part of the programming.

b) literals

Literals are also known as constants in programming. These are values that can be assigned to a variable using an assignment operator. All literals can be replaced if wanted. Strings also fall under literals and can often be manipulated using different system functions.

Here is an example

a = 355

Here 355 is the literal that is being assigned to the variable 'a'

c) Variables

Variables are used as memory storage to store an assignment literal and use them whenever needed. Variables are important when dealing with functions and logical statements. You can easily change an assigned variable using logical statements.

Here is an example

first = 3

Here first is the name of the variable and 3 is the literal value that has been assigned to the variable. Always remember that variable can be assigned only through an assignment statement.

d) Datatypes

Datatypes are used to categorize variables that are created. It is important to assign a specified memory location whenever a variable is created. However, it is not feasible to create a constant size of memory location every time. So while creating a variable it is important to specify a data type. There are a lot of default data types such as integer, float, double and character.

Here is an example

int a=4788

// Here int is the data type

e) Conditional statements

Programming is composed of logical statements. When dealing with complex code we need to use control flow statements to get desired results. Python offers a lot of control flow statements such as conditionals and loops.

Conditional is a control flow statement where we have an option to choose by a logical evaluation. If—else is an easy way to represent a conditional statement.

Here is an example:

if(a>3)

{ #print the statement}

else

{ #pront another statement}

f) Operators

Operators are used to combine the statements to form expressions. In the previous chapter, we have in detail discussed the operator module. Always make sure you are aware of operator precedence before debugging the code.

g) Strings

Strings are one of the most important data types in python. Usually, we deal with a lot of string literals in common. Datasets are often combined in strong notions and can be manipulated using some of the string functions that are provided to python by default.

here is an example:

a = " This is a strong"

a.tolowercase()

Using this system function, you can convert string literals into lower case. You can check the documentation to find out different available string functions.

h) Exceptions

Python also provides advanced exception handling mechanism to deal with errors. Programs usually encounter errors while they are running. It is important to show the errors to the end-user to help them understand the mistake they are doing.

To make this happen we use try, catch blocks to enter the exceptions and their error output.

i) Lists

Python handles multiple data using the available structures. There are different data structures such as lists, tulles, and dictionaries to handle multi-dimensional data. It is important to master these if you are trying to develop machine learning applications.

With this, we have explained some of the basic programmatically concepts that are necessary to start coding in Python. In the next section, we will in detail discuss coding using an IDE.

How to start coding in Python?

In the previous chapter, we have explained about using a text editor to create python programs. However, python programs can be written using an Integrated development environment. In this section, we use PyCharm to explain about starting to code with Python.

Step 1:

Open the software and click on the "create new" button to open a new python file. You can even create new classes and interfaces for easy maintenance of the python project.

Step 2:

After creating a new python file, you can start writing code. In the IDE you can easily insert conditionals and loops using different pre-installed functions. You can also create templates and packages on a one click

Step3:

After creating a program, it is now time to start compiling in the IDE. You can just click on the Run button to start the Python interpreter to look at your code. If any errors are present, they will be displayed.

Step 4:

You can interlink these individual codes to start creating packages. You can use inheritance to use methods that have been used by python classes

Step 5:

Click the save button to save all the code information that has been created.

What should you remember?

Always, make sure that you are following the Python programming conditions. Python doesn't support case sensitive statements and there is no use of indentation spaces. Python is also easy to maintain and organize. However, we recommend you maintain a good coding structure to help you look back at your code without any confusion.

With this, we have completed a brief introduction to starting code with Python. There are a lot of resources to further enhance your skills. You can look at our book in this previous module to increase your Python programming knowledge.

In the next chapter, we will start discussing a sample project.

Let us go!

Chapter 10: Planning and design a project in Python

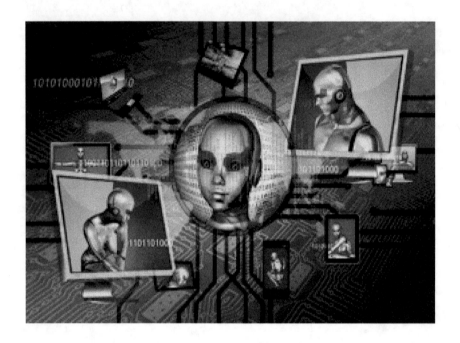

In the previous chapter, we have learned about basic programming structures. This chapter will help you know how to start creating a project with an example.

This chapter and the next chapter are practical experimentation with a sample project to increase your Python skills.

Follow along!

Know the purpose of your project

Before developing the project, first introduce the purpose of the project, so that everyone will focus on it when studying.

The development objectives of this project are as follows:

(1) Write a project to remotely control the computer to do a remote shutdown or restart.

(2) Review the basic knowledge of Python that you have learned before.

(3) Master the general process of project development. When receiving a software project, one should not blindly do it immediately but should do it step by step according to the process of project development.

Project making procedure

Developing a project from scratch is a complex procedure and is often achieved only when certain procedures are followed. A lot of experienced programmers use the following blueprint we are going to use now to develop Python projects. The process is mainly as follows.

(1) Demand analysis.

(2) Design.

(3) Writing.

(4) Testing.

(5) Use.

(6) Maintenance.

If you don't know these steps, get a project and do it according to your feelings. Large projects will inevitably be done in a chaotic way, which will eventually affect the efficiency of project development and the ultimate benefits.

When developing a project, the development steps are very important. Everyone should start from small projects and form good and standard habits.

【OBJ】 Concept of Demand Analysis

Requirement analysis is a detailed analysis of the functions to be required by a project. For example, the purpose, scope, definition, and function of a project are analyzed, in other words, the requirements of the project are positioned.

Application Examples of Requirement Analysis for this Project

This project is to make a Python small software that can remotely control restart or shutdown functions of a computer. The programming idea is as follows. First, you need to know how to control the restart and shutdown of the computer locally through Python, and then you need to know how to send messages to Python programs remotely.

Here, Python's standard library can be used to control the restart or shutdown of the local computer. To achieve remote control, e-mail can be used as a remote-control channel. For example, Python can automatically log into the mailbox to detect mail.

When sending a shutdown command to this mailbox, if Python detects a shutdown command, Python directly sends a command to control the shutdown of the machine.

The so-called "requirement analysis" here refers to functional requirement analysis, that is, clarifying which functions the project needs to realize.

Secondly, this is not a complete requirement analysis document, but a draft requirement analysis during actual development.

This step is very necessary and it is recommended to master it.

For a complete requirement analysis document, you can search the corresponding template on the search engine for reference and compilation.

If it is not commercial software development, writing a complete requirement analysis document is not a necessary step.

The following is a brief demand analysis of the project:

(1) Control the shutdown of the local computer through Python code.

(2) Log into the mailbox through Python (of course, other remote-control channels can also be selected).

(3) Monitor and read the mail content of the designated mailbox through Python.

(4) Realize the function of mail sending through Python.

(5) The core business logic processing part (such as how to monitor, if judge when to shut down or restart, etc.).

After understanding the above functional requirements, the corresponding code can be written step by step.

⌜OBJ⌟ Implementation of Simple Code

As mentioned above, to restart or shut down the computer remotely, Python must first control the computer to restart or shut down locally.

The following is the realization of this function. For the first time, only Python can control the computer to restart or shut down locally.

This development is also called the first development and can be used as the first version of the simple program in the development process of small software.

If you want to control the local computer to restart or shut down, you can use the os.system () method and pass in relevant Shell instructions.

You can control the computer to shut down through a Shell command shutdown, and you can also control the computer to restart through a Shell command ' -r'.

Here is the Python code:

import os

☐# shutdown the system

os.system{ Enter the parameters here}

After executing the above code, the computer will automatically shut down.

If you want to use Python code to control the restart of your local computer, you can do this by following Python code:

import os

restart the system

os.r(Enter the parameters here)

After executing the above code, the computer will restart automatically.

Therefore, the simple version of the code is as follows:

{Use import functions here}

("Please enter what you want to do: shutdown input 1, restart input 2")

Note 1 enclosed in double quotation marks.

Because the input is a string instead of the number

if (result = = "1"):

shut down { Get the parameters here}

 print ("shutdown instruction is ready")

```
elif (result = = "2"):

# Restart os.system { Get the parameters here}

print ("restart instruction is ready")

else:

print ("no operation performed")
```

After executing the above program, we will be prompted to enter the desired operation, as follows:

Please enter the operation you wish to perform:

shutdown

input 1,

restart

input 2

If we want to shut down, we can enter 1 and press enter.

If you want to restart, you can enter 2 and press Enter.

If you enter additional information and press enter, nothing will be done.

For example, entering 3 and pressing enter key will output the following information:

Please enter what you want to do:

shut down

input 1,

restart input 2

If you enter 2 and press Enter, the restart command will be executed as follows:

Please enter the operation you wish to perform:

shutdown input 1 and restart input 22.

The restart command was executed successfully.

Subsequently, the computer will be shut down and restarted automatically within one minute.

Similarly, if after executing the above code, enter 1 and press enter key, the shutdown operation will be executed.

Here, how to control the restart and shutdown of the local computer through Python code is realized.

This is the first version of the small target software, i.e. the simple version.

The final target has not been reached, so further development is needed.

[OBJ] Debugging during Development

Sometimes, when writing software, there will be certain errors and problems. The process of trying to solve these problems is called debugging.

When we develop this project, we will also encounter various problems. It doesn't matter.

We just need to find out where the problem is and improve the corresponding procedures. Debugging is often carried out during project development, and it is difficult to develop the program perfectly at one time.

For example, when you write a program in the mail reading phase if the waiting time for the operation is too long, you will often encounter some errors that cannot be connected. At this time, you can solve the problem by re-executing the login code.

This process is a debugging process.

Similarly, when you encounter other problems, you should try your best to locate the problem first, and then compare with the above procedures, carefully observe which place or details the problem is.

If you still can't think out, you can put the error prompt into the search engine to find out and see if it can be solved.

In short, when you encounter problems, think independently and try to solve these problems independently can make your programming ability stronger.

⌊OBJ⌋ Concept of Program Packaging

The process of turning the written program code into software that can be directly executed is called program packaging.

For example, scripts written now can only be run in the Python editor.

After they are packaged into software, they can be run directly in the operating system without the support of the Python editor.

Method of Packaging Python Programs

Readers can use some tools to package Python programs into executable application software.

In Python, tools commonly used for packaging include py2exe, Pyinstaller, etc. These tools do not need to be mastered completely, so everyone can choose a tool that they think is suitable.

This book will introduce how to package Python programs through Pyinstaller.To use Pyinstaller, you need to install it first.

Here, you can install Pyinstaller directly using pip. First, open the cmd command-line interface, and then enter the instructions. The Pyinstaller is installed through the "pip install pyinstaller" instruction and only needs to wait for the installation to be completed.

After the installation is completed, the installation success prompt message will appear.

In addition, readers can see the installed tool file pyinstaller.exe in the Scripts directory under the Python installation directory.

▢Next, you can use the Pyinstaller tool to package Python programs into application software.

For example, the path of the complete program of this project is "D:/ sample/project.py" and the Python installation directory of my computer is "D:/Python". Therefore, the Python program of this project can be packaged through the following cmd instructions:

D: \ > d: \ python\ scripts \installer

d: \sample\ project.py

▢The successfully packaged executable program can be found in the D:/dist directory. The sample folder is the software folder related to the project.py program that has just been packaged and generated.

▢The file with the ".exe" extension is the executable file generated after packaging. Double-click the file to run directly.

At this time, the current computer can be remotely controlled to restart or shut down only by opening the program, so long as the "shutdown" or "restart" instruction is sent to the designated mailbox.

As can be seen, the currently packaged program needs to rely on many files. Because there are too many dependent files, it is very inconvenient to migrate packaged programs to other computers to run.

In fact, it is also possible to package all the dependent files into an. exe file, just add the -F parameter when packaging.

At the same time, a cmd interface will appear after the software is opened. In some cases, you don't want the software to have this cmd interface, but you can also directly shield it through the -w parameter when packaging, which will be much more beautiful in some cases.

Next, I will show you how to package all the dependent files into a .exe file without the cmd interface.

The packaged cmd instructions are as follows:

After packaging, a separate. exe file will be generated in the D:/dist directory. Readers can directly migrate the file to other computers.

Even if other computers do not have a good Python development environment, double-click the. exe file to execute it (but it is better to close the antivirus software to avoid interference from accidental killing).

In addition, since the -w parameter is added during packaging, the cmd interface will not be displayed when running the software, because the cmd interface has been shielded by the -w parameter.

If you want to display a cmd interface, do not add -w parameter when packing. Running the software can realize the function of remotely controlling the computer to shut down or restart through e-mail.

With this, we have completed a brief introduction to Python project creation.

In the next chapter, we will further discuss this practical project.

Follow along!

Chapter 11: Practical Project in python

In the previous chapter, we have discussed ways to design a project. In this project, we will in detail explanation about the implementation of a practical project with a lot of background information followed by Python code.

Follow along carefully.

Maintenance and Improvement

⧈It has been successfully implemented to control the shutdown or restart of the computer through Python, but it cannot meet all requirements. Therefore, it is necessary to solve this defect: the program can not only control the shutdown or restart of the local computer but also remotely control the shutdown or restart of the computer through the network.

After discovering the defects of the old version, the process of developing the new version is the maintenance and improvement of the software.

[OBJ] *Remote Control Channel*

⬚If you want to remotely control the shutdown or restart of the computer, the local computer needs networking. After networking, you also need to choose a remote-control channel, such as Gmail, web page or e-mail.

Controlling Python to Operate Computer 1 via Mail

As long as it can communicate with remote, it can be used as a channel for remote control. Therefore, there are many channels for remote control. In this project, the mail is chosen as the channel tool for remote control.

[OBJ] *Controlling Python to Operate Computer 2 via Mail*

This project uses e-mail as a remote-control channel to realize remote control of computers. It can be seen that the user sends corresponding instructions to the e-mail, then the instructions are transmitted to Python code (the specified instructions can be monitored regularly by Python), and finally, the local computer is controlled to execute corresponding operations by Python code.

Therefore, the following parts need to be developed in turn:

(1) Log into the mailbox through Python (of course, other remote-control channels can also be selected).

(2) Monitor and read the mail content of the designated mailbox through Python.

(3) Realize the function of mail sending through Python (not required).

(4) the core business logic processing part.

First of all, you need to prepare a mailbox. Because the port and use of Gmail are different from other mailboxes, here you can use Rediff mail for operation.

Here, the author has prepared a Rediff mailbox (account number or password may be modified later, and the modified code cannot be used, so everyone should register a mailbox of their own).

Account number: example@rediffmail.com

Password: sample123

Log in to your mailbox on the web page and make some settings.

The default SMTP and POP3 are closed, but SMTP is required to send mail through Python code, POP3 is required to read mail through Python code, so these two items need to be opened first.

You can select the "Settings-Client pop/imap/smtp" option in the mailbox personal center control panel.

As you can see, the default POP3 and SMTP are turned off, so you need to select the "on" radio button and save it.

⯑After opening, you can log in to the mailbox using Python code.

As can be seen, the default POP3 server and SMTP server information of Rediff mailbox are as follows.

POP3 server: pop.rediff.com.

SMTP Server: smtp.rediff.com.

Next, I'll show you how to log in to your mailbox using the Python code.

The purpose of logging into the mailbox is different, and the modules used are also different.

If the purpose of logging into the mailbox is to send mail, you can call SMTP () under smtplib to establish a mail object, and then call login () method under the mail object to log in.

If the purpose of logging into the mailbox is to check mail, you can call POP3 () under poplib to establish a mail object, and then call the user () method and pass_ () method under the object to set the account and password when logging into the mailbox. After setting, you can log in.

Next, you can enter the following code to demonstrate how to log in to the mailbox:

The key parts have been commented:

1. log in to the mailbox for sending mail

import { Enter the library}

establish a mail object through SMTP (), the parameters in which are the SMTP server address of the corresponding mailbox

smpt.call()

Through the above exercises, everyone should have mastered how to log into the mailbox using Python code. It should be noted that the modules and methods used to log in to the mailbox are different depending on the purpose of use.

Next, I'll show you how to monitor and read the mail content of the specified mailbox through Python.

If you want to read the mail information of the specified mailbox through Python code, you need to log in to the corresponding mailbox through POP3 first, then call stat () to obtain statistical information.

You can specify to return the first few lines of mail information through top () and decode the returned information.

After decoding, the decoded information can be converted into recognizable mail information by email.message_from_string (), and then the recognizable mail information can be processed by email.header.decode_header (), and the required mail information can be read out after processing.

For example, if you need to read the title of the latest email, it can be implemented by the following code, and the key parts have been given detailed comments:

```
print (statistics) (Here is the values)

emailmsg = mail. top (statistics [0], 0)

print(emailmsg)

for I in emailmsg [1]: newmsg. append (I.decode ())

> > > # view decoded information >

title = decode _ header (myemailmsg ["subject"])
```

Through the above code, the mail information can be read directly. At this time, you can log into the mailbox of the webpage version to verify whether it is correct.

After logging into the mailbox of the webpage version, you can see the information on the latest email.

It can be seen that the message title of the latest mail is "I am a test mail", which is consistent with the results read and output in the code. Therefore, the mail information in the mailbox has now been successfully read through the code.

Next, let's introduce how to realize the function of mail sending through Python. This part of the program is not necessary for this project.

The purpose of this project is to realize the remote control of the computer through the remote channel of e-mail, which only requires Python to monitor the instruction information in the e-mail.

The link to sending e-mail can be realized by Python code or traditional e-mail, so this part is not necessary. Of course, learning the function of this part and writing it in the program can make the project more perfect.

If you need to realize the function of mail sending through Python, you can log in to the e-mail box by SMTP first, then set the content of the e-mail to be sent through MIMEText under email.mime.text, then call sendmail () under the logged-in e-mail object to realize the mail sending, and finally call close () under the e-mail object to realize the connection closing.

For example, the following code can be used to send e-mail messages:

mail.login ('credentials',' password') (235, B' ok authenticated')

content = mimetext ('I am the specific content of the mail! This email is mainly used to test whether it can be sent. ")

content ['from'] =' sample@rediffmail.com'

content ['to'] =' example@rediffmail.com, abcdefg'

After running the above code, the mail is sent to the specified mailbox through Python code. At this time, the receiver's mailbox will display the relevant email information just sent.

It can be seen that the relevant mail has been received in the receiver's mailbox. If you can't find it in your inbox, you can try to find it in the trash.

To avoid entering the trash, you can add the sender's email address to the white list.

Now, the related functions can be realized through Python code. Next, we will integrate the above functions to complete the development of the whole project.

At present, the core business logic processing part of this project is written. The main idea is: firstly, establish a function to control the shutdown of the local computer, a function to control the restart of the local computer, a function to read the header of the first email of the designated email, a function to send the corresponding content to the designated email, etc.

Then write a while loop in which you log in to the specified email regularly and read the header of the first email.

If the title is certain specified information, the corresponding custom function is called to perform the corresponding operation, for example, the title is "shutdown", and the shutdown function can be called to control the shutdown of the local computer.

After performing the corresponding operation, call the mail sending function to send a new mail to the specified mailbox. It should be avoided that the title of the new mail is the same as the specified information defined by us.

In this way, when the software monitors the title of the latest mail in the mailbox next time, it will not perform the previous operation endlessly, because the title of the latest mail has been reset at this time.

The complete code of this project is as follows:

Defrestart (): importos

restart os.system ('shutdown-r')

print ("restart command executed successfully")

mail = poplib.pop3 ('pop.rediff.com') mail.user ('weiweitest789 @ rediff.com')

detect time.sleep (5) every 5s

While the program is running, wait for remote instructions.

As long as the above program is executed on the local computer, the computer will always listen to remote instructions. For example, the computer in the home runs the above program now, but you are in the office.

At this time, you can send an email titled "Restart" to weiweitest789@rediff.com (that is, the email address monitored in the program), and the computer in the home will automatically restart. If you send an email titled "Shut Down" to the email, the computer in the home will automatically shut down. At this time, you can remotely control the computer to restart or shut down.

For example, now send a message titled "Shut Down" remotely to the email address (weiweitest789@rediff.com) monitored in the program. While the program is running, wait for the remote instruction shutdown instruction to execute successfully.

Then the computer automatically performs the shutdown operation.

After rebooting, log in to the receiving mailbox and find the mail message. The mail titled "shutdown" was just sent manually and remotely. when the local program detects the title "shutdown", it automatically calls the send () function to send a reset mail, i.e. the mail titled "test" and then controls the computer to perform the shutdown operation. So far, this project has been successfully written and its functions have been realized.

[OBJ] Project Implementation and Summary

So far, this project has been fully realized. In the process of writing this small project, everyone knew the basic process of project development and went through it completely. I hope everyone will have a project management awareness when receiving software projects.

Developing projects according to standard procedures will greatly improve the development efficiency of large projects. You these ideas to develop your projects in Python. All the best!

In the next chapter, we will in detail discuss Machine learning.

Let us go!

Chapter 12: Machine learning in Python

Machine learning is a branch of computer science that extracts valuable information from the huge chunks of data that is available. It uses various computer science and statistics principles to create a well versed artificial intelligent application.

Machine learning has been a prominent field in research for decades.

However, in the 21st century with the development of high-level computing machines, Machine learning applications rose into an all-time high. Almost all web applications use Machine learning algorithms to suggest recommendations for the user.

This chapter is a detailed step-by-step material that will help you understand the importance of Machine learning in day-to-day life and will also introduce you to using Python as a supportive language to develop Machine learning applications.

Follow along!

Machine learning in Day-to-Day life

Before starting with the technical stuff, we will give a real-world example to help you understand the importance of machine learning algorithms in real life.

Imagine using a virtual assistant such as Siri/Google Assistant to ask your questions regarding the best restaurant in your surroundings. When you ask this question, the virtual assistant analyzes huge data that is present and selects a restaurant according to your requirements. This is how an actual search query works. Machine learning adds a layer of functionality to it. It monitors how you have reacted to the result and improves itself and produces better results the next time.

So, to say in a single sentence:

" Machine learning is a computer learning scenario where the machine improves itself with time"

Applications of Machine Learning

At the initial stages, Machine learning is used to automate decision making with the help of various algorithms that have been developed by then. This exact branch of machine learning is known as supervised learning.

There is also another branch of machine learning known as unsupervised learning where the machine generates new algorithms by itself according to the datasets provided.

For example, Machine learning algorithms are used to develop Spam filter mails in the 2000s. Mail developers used all the spam words that they have collected and made an algorithm to automatically send the suspected mail to the spam folder.

You may wonder that this is just a normal spam filter application but this spam filter software automatically updates itself with the new spam filter database.

Machine learning systems learn all the way while doing the work they are told to do.

In the next section, we will in detail discuss the applications of Machine learning in detail.

Follow along!

a) They are used in Medical clinical analysis

Machine learning can be used to develop applications that can detect the medical tumor or the skin diseases that patients are suffering by checking the thousands of clinical photos that are collected. They can also be used to conduct a differential diagnosis for the patient at the same time.

b) Security

Machine learning can be used to develop applications that can increase the security of online transactions. A lot of fraudulent credit card operations follow a pattern and it is often easy by machine learning algorithms to block the fraudulent transactions.

c) Image processing

Machine learning can be used to develop applications that can detect your face. This branch of machine learning is known as Deep learning and is quite famous among the industry.

d) Recommendations

A lot of websites rely on cloud user data to give the same recommendations that the users may like. E-commerce websites Like amazon analyze the user data and provide recommendations that the users may likely buy. All these recommendations are generated using different machine learning algorithms that the websites use.

5) Categorizing

Machine learning algorithms can also be used to categorize the data that is collected using different topics. This is known as the regression algorithm and can be very useful if done in the right way for e-commerce and streaming applications.

With this, we have completed a brief introduction that explains the application of Machine learning. In the next section, we will discuss the usage of Python in Machine learning applications.

Let us go!

Why Python is considered best for Machine Learning?

Python is considered best because it consists of libraries for every available computer stream. There are libraries for statistics and visualization that can be explicitly used for data analysis. Python also is very interactive and can interact with the data points using software such as Jupyter notebook. Also, remember that machine learning is a computational process that highly depends on the iteration levels. Python is an interactive language and is thus considered the best programming language for machine learning.

Here are some of the Python libraries that are essential for developing Machine learning Projects.

a) Scikit Learn

This is a fundamental machine learning library consisting of different famous machine learning algorithms. Scikit learn consists of a documentation file where there is sufficient information about every algorithm that is present.

It is particularly famous among computer scientists because it curates a lot of essential algorithms in one library.

A lot of machine learning algorithms present in scipy can be easily deployed to your software.

First of all, install the scikit learn in your system using the following command:

root @ tony : pipi install { Enter the dependencies} scikit

What are the dependencies that are required?

You need to install Anaconda a Python module for making sci-kit learn work.

Anaconda consists of a lot of Python modules that are essential to run machine learning algorithms.

b) Jupyter notebook

This is a python tool that will help you to run the program code in the browser.

It is important to note that Jupyter also supports different languages. So, if you have any code of other languages you can integrate it with python to get desirable results.

C) NumPy

As said before, Machine learning is a branch of computer science that is a combination of mathematics, statistics and computer science.

To make efficient machine learning programs it is essential to use statistical algorithms that NumPy offers. NumPy is a python library that consists of multidimensional arrays and higher-order mathematical functions. NumPy is usually used to represent or find out data points in the data set.

d) SciPy

Machine learning in the initial stages is a complete scientific field. A lot of algorithms are developed to find out an easy way to deal with programming high computing machines. SciPy is a python library that deals with scientific computing. It is important because it consists of higher-order mathematical functions that can be used in deep learning applications. SciPy modules can also be used to create sparse matrices.

e) matplotlib

It is important to visualize the data while developing machine learning applications. A lot of statistical graphs can be used to create visualization such as histograms and scatters. Data set can be visualized using the matplotlib in Python. This library can help you to provide an interactive environment while dealing with huge chunks of data.

f) pandas

Data analysis is also a branch of machine learning and requires pandas to analyze the data by using data frames. Using pandas, you can create programs that can query and select the data.

It is important to master pandas to analyze CSV files.

These are some of the important Python libraries that are essential to master machine learning.

It is also important to remember that Python 3 is mandatory to run all of these libraries mentioned. So, make sure you are aware of all the Python 3 programming basics.

In the next section, we will explain a simple example that will help you understand the process of machine learning.

It is quite theoretical for now. However, you can always fill your gaps with research.

Python is still iterating and is not forward compatible, which also causes the current Python to split into two major versions, namely Python 2.X and Python 3.x.

Although it is not yet grammatically two languages, the two codes cannot be mixed, and the choice of the version is also the first thing to be determined when learning to use Python.

Previously, it was generally believed that Python 2.X had a longer development time and more and more mature support libraries in various aspects. many people recommended starting with this version.

However, as the Python team announced that it would stop maintaining Python 2.X in 2020, all major communities have already started the migration from 2.X to 3.X, so it is more recommended to choose 3.X when learning Python now.

Python is a general programming language, and its syntax satisfies Turing completeness, which cannot be fully explained here. However, if you are familiar with the C or Java language, you can think of Python's syntax as a highly condensed version of them. In addition to the above-mentioned need not make type declarations, Python also lacks curly braces to indicate scope and semicolons at the end of statements.

At the same time, the indentation in Python is not only a code specification but also a mandatory requirement at the syntax level.

If you have a language foundation and remember these differences, you should be able to use Python skillfully and quickly.

Strategy for learning Machine learning with Python

Generally speaking, there are two ways to practice algorithm theory. One is to implement the algorithm with code by oneself. The other is to make full use of the convenience of the tool, quickly understand and grasp the existing resources, and then begin to solve practical problems.

I think it is very difficult to decide on whether to build wheels again. Each method has its advantages and disadvantages.

After the rapid development of machine learning in recent years, it has accumulated very rich open resources.

By making full use of these resources, you can quickly master and solve practical problems even if you did not know this field before.

First is the programming language, we choose Python. In the past few years, Python and R languages have maintained a dual situation in the field of machine learning.

It can be generally considered that the industry prefers Python while academia prefers R.

However, with the development of technology, Python language has become the undisputed "eldest brother" in the field of machine learning, especially after the support library required for in-depth learning in recent years has been implemented in Python without exception.

Due to the popularity of machine learning, Python even has the strength to compete with the traditional programming languages C and Java and tends to lag in the ranking of many programming languages.

The next step is to support the library Numpy. Machine learning involves a large number of mathematical operations such as matrix operations.

Fortunately, Python has two major characteristics, one is flexibility, and the other is a large number of libraries. Numpy is a professional support library specially designed for scientific computing in Python and is well-known in the industry.

Not only machine learning, but also other scientific fields such as mathematical operations involved in astrophysics, either directly use NumPy or build higher-level functional libraries based on NumPy.

Finally, is the algorithm library Scikit-Learn. There are many Python-based machine learning algorithm libraries. However, Scikit-Learn is always at the top of the list.

It not only has a complete range of types but also can find the corresponding API for the machine learning algorithms available on the market. It is simply a "supermarket of machine learning algorithms". Besides, it is well packaged and has a clear structure.

You can complete the call of a complex algorithm through a few simple lines of code. It is a good introduction to the field of machine learning, and it is also an advanced magic weapon.

Famous Machine Learning Algorithms

Common machine learning algorithms are as follows:

(1) Linear Regression Algorithm

This is the most basic machine learning algorithm, but although sparrows are small and have all five organs, this algorithm can be called the "Hello World" program in the field of machine learning algorithms. It uses linear methods to solve regression problems.

(2) Logistic regression classification algorithm

This is the "twin brother" of the linear regression algorithm. Its core idea is still the linear method, but a "waistcoat" named Logistic function is set up, which enables it to solve classification problems.

(3) KNN classification algorithm

This algorithm is the only one of the classification algorithms introduced in this book that does not rely on mathematical or statistical models but purely relies on "life experience".

It solves the classification problem through the idea of "finding the nearest neighbor". Its core idea has a far-reaching relationship with the consensus mechanism in blockchain technology.

(4) Naive Bayesian classification algorithm

This is a set of algorithms that can refresh your world outlook. It believes that the results are not deterministic but probabilistic. What you see in front of your eyes is only the results with the greatest probability.

Of course, the algorithm is used to solve the problem. Naive Bayesian classification algorithm solves the classification problem.

(5) Support Vector Machine Classification Algorithm

If the Logistic regression classification algorithm is the most basic linear classification algorithm, then the support vector machine is the highest form of linear classification algorithm and is also the most "mathematical" machine learning algorithm. The algorithm uses a series of stunning mathematical techniques to map linearly indivisible data points into linearly separable data points and then uses the simplest linear method to solve the problem.

(6)K-means clustering algorithm

Supervised learning is a mainstream method of machine learning at present, but sample marking needs a lot of labor costs, which is prone to the problem of large sample accumulation scale but insufficient marking. Unsupervised learning is a machine learning algorithm that does not rely on labeled samples.

(7) Neural Network Classification Algorithm

Many people think that this algorithm is bionic, and the object of imitation is our brain. The neural network classification algorithm is also the starting point of the popular depth learning algorithm.

With this, we have completed a thorugh introduction to machine learning using Python.

In the next chapter, we will in detail discuss about classes and objects in Python.

Follow along!

Chapter 13: How to create a Class in python?

Object-oriented programming is an essential feature in the Python programming language. Even with the presence of the functional programming paradigm in Python a lot of developers like to use object-oriented mechanisms for developing programs.

There are a lot of reasons that make developers choose object-oriented programming over functional. Machine learning experts should be quite aware of object and class creation when dealing with algorithms.

This chapter is a comprehensive introduction to object-oriented programming basics.

Let us start!

How is it different from procedural programming?

Procedural programming is a paradigm where problems are solved using reusable code segments known as functions. It is often difficult to insert new logic or data to the already created code. In a machine learning environment, it is often important to automatically rearrange the code segments to give the best results.

This is the reason why machine learning enthusiasts should implement resources that will help you to extend into an object-oriented model whenever needed.

How does object orientation work?

Object-oriented programming uses a different philosophy that separates like-minded objects into categories. Using these categories, you can individually change functionalities that are required.

Apart from easier code maintenance, they can also be used to maintain the unity of the functions.

We will now in detail discuss classes and objects from a data scientist perspective.

What are Classes and Objects?

From a programmer's perspective, classes are a blueprint that are developed to deal with objects easily.

In a class, we will usually group like-minded variables, methods, and constructors to easily work with them.

When dealing with small projects procedural programming techniques are feasible.

However, as the size of the project expands, we need to write a lot of code that does the same thing from a different perspective.

To counter this problem Classes and Objects are developed, by which we can easily inherit the parent classes and use them in our projects.

What do classes consist of?

Classes consist of methods that can do a certain task. There are global and local variables in a class that can be used according to the situation.

All these methods and variables can be used as an object instance by the programmer.

How to define a class?

In Python, unlike Java, you need to store classes using a Python file. In java programming language programmers usually save separate class files with a .class extension. However, Python makes things simple by using the same .py format. In the next section, we will use an example that will help you understand the creation of a class in Python.

To master object-oriented programming, we first need to understand the basic theories and concepts of object-oriented programming.

This section will introduce the basic theories and concepts of object-oriented programming in detail.

Object-Oriented scenarios in real life

In the world we live in, any specific thing can be regarded as an object, and each object can handle some things or have some static characteristics.

For example, each specific person can be regarded as an object. This object can handle some things, such as eating, singing, writing, etc.

Some functions realized by this object can be called methods of this object. Similarly, this object has some static features, such as hair, arms, body, etc. You can call the static features of this object the attributes of this object.

Thus, the method is dynamic and the attribute is static.

If Tony is regarded as an object A and Christopher as object b, Tony and Christopher can communicate and pass on some information. In the object-oriented thinking method, messages can also be transmitted and communicated between objects, so that each object can form a powerful and complex network, thus realizing some complex architectures and functions.

According to the commonness of various objects in nature, objects can be abstracted into classes, and any object must belong to a certain class. Objects are concrete and classes are abstract.

For example, there are now the following objects:

Object A: Tony is a person.

Object B: Tony

Object C: A specific orange

Object d: A specific apple

According to the commonness between object a and object b, object a and object b can be abstracted as human, which is called human for short.

According to the commonness between object c and object d, object c and object d can be abstracted as fruit class.

Thus, objects A, B, C and D all have their own classes. Of course, the commonness among object A, object B, object C, and object D can also be extracted and abstracted into a class of biology.

In object-oriented programming, we can divide a complex software into various required classes according to requirements, and then write various methods and attributes.

When it is used specifically, it can be instantiated into specific objects directly according to the class, and then relevant functions can be implemented.

The process of instantiation is the process of transforming abstract things into concrete things. After instantiation, the software's relatively complex architecture and functions can be implemented using related objects.

It can be seen that programming through object-oriented thinking can make the development of programs closer to the real world and realize complex functions and architectures more convenient.

Advanced Concepts

Through the above introduction, I believe everyone has a simple understanding of the basic idea of object-oriented, and this section will specifically introduce how to apply the object-oriented method to program design.

For example, to realize a large project, you can divide the project into different components, treat each different component as each class, then program these components separately, and finally assemble each component into a large project.

This approach can control the project as a whole and make the development of the project more efficient.

Object-oriented programming is different from process-oriented programming. Process-oriented programming is to write programs according to the specific process of this project. This method is suitable for writing small and medium-sized programs, while for larger projects, it can be handled with object-oriented thinking.

If large projects are also developed according to the process-oriented programming idea, the efficiency will be lower and the object-oriented programming idea will be used for development.

It is only necessary to divide the project into various classes (i.e. abstract forms of various parts of large projects), then develop various classes, and then combine various classes.

When you need to use it, you can directly create specific objects according to classes, and then implement corresponding specific functions through each object.

Class is a relatively important concept in object-oriented, and object is also a relatively important concept in object-oriented.

The concepts of class and object are usually mentioned together, and this section will show you how to use Python to implement classes and objects.

How to create classes?

Classes are abstractions of commonness between certain objects.

In popular terms, a class is a synthesis of many identical things. For example, a good song, a piece of calligraphy and a good-looking novel are all the objects.

You can think about the commonness of these things and what can be used to summarize them?

They can be summarized by a class called "literature and art". Literature and art do not represent any specific thing, it is an abstract concept.

In a word: class is the abstraction of an object, and the object is the concrete expression of class, which is also called the instance of the class.

For example, as we have just introduced, the objects of a beautiful song, calligraphy, and a beautiful novel can abstract the category of literature and art.

When we say literature and art, it must be abstract, so the category is abstract of the object.

Use of Classes in Python

In Python, if you want to implement object-oriented programming, you first need to divide the corresponding classes and then write the specific code to implement the classes.

If you want to create a class in Python, you can do this in the following format:

Class Name ():

{

  Enter the implementation procedure here

}

For example, if you want to create a human class, you can do this by following the code:

class man:

▢pass

Here, the pass statement has no practical significance but is called a placeholder statement to ensure the integrity of the program.

After running the above program, we can make the following input:

>>> print（man）

As you can see, the current corresponding output result is "class ......", indicating that man is a class at this time.

Application Examples of Objects

Generally speaking, classes cannot be directly used to implement related functions and operations, because classes are abstract.

At this time, the corresponding class will generally be instantiated into the corresponding object, and then relevant functions and operations will be implemented through the corresponding object.

In Python, the format for instantiating a class as an object is as follows:

Object {Enter the name here} = Class Name (You can enter your parameters here)

As you can see, if you want to instantiate the class, you just need to add parentheses after the class name.

For example, the class man defined above can be instantiated as a vehicle's object by the following code:

class man:

☐pass

vehicle=man()

As you can see, when instantiating, you only need to follow the corresponding format described above.

Run the above program, and then make the following debugging input:

>>> print （vehicle）

This is an object

#"A36FA90"

It can be found that when vehicle is output, the result is "...object...", where object means vehicle is initiated, while "A36FA90" in the above output result is the specific storage space of vehicle.

It is worth noting that there may be multiple objects under the same class, that is, multiple different objects can be instantiated based on one class. Several different objects may have some common features and functions, but they represent different individuals. For example, under the human class, not only the object vehicle can be instantiated, but also car and bus can be instantiated.

Although vehicle, car, and bus have some common features or methods, such as having the function of eating and having the characteristics of hair, body, etc. (because they are instantiated based on the same class), these objects represent different individuals and are different. Modifying the object vehicle will not affect other objects such as car and bus.

We might as well follow the program running above and enter the following code for demonstration:

> > create this object

> > vehicle = man ()

> > create this object

> > car = man ()

> > view information about these objects

⬚>>> print(car)

>>>> print(vehicle)

Therefore, the two objects belong to different individuals, and communication between the two objects is possible, but there is no inevitable influence.

With this, we have completed a brief introduction to classes in Python.

In the next chapter, we will in detail discuss about loops. Follow along!

Chapter 14: How to create Loops in python?

Machine learning often relies on repeating a task until it becomes a perfect sample for the query. To significantly achieve these results in Python we need to effectively use Loops. Python offers a variety of loop structures in their libraries.

In this chapter, we will in detail discuss various loops using examples.

Let us do it!

What is a Loop?

To say in simple words Loop is a programming structure that can repeat a task as many times you need. You can control the number of times a structure can loop using different logical evaluations.

In this chapter, we will in detail discuss for and while loop with examples.

Before discussing in detail about Loops we suggest you understand the concept of Judgement in control flow statements adequately. Judgment is a layman concept that processes the logical entity only when the conditions are met.

If the conditions are not met then the program either stops or destroys by itself.

In real life example, we can use traffic lights to help you understand this fundamental concept that is necessary to understand looping structures.

You can't cross the road when a red light is shown because it is the condition that needs to be followed. Judgment is also essentially used in conditional and case statements.

However, in this chapter, we will only discuss looping structures.

Follow along!

while statement

The while statement in Python is mainly used to control the repeated execution of a statement.

The basic usage format of the while statement is as follows:

While (Enter the logical value)

{

   Enter the statements;

}

Among them, the else clause part can be omitted if it is not needed.

How to use While statement?

The while statement is very convenient to use. For example, you want to repeatedly output "I like This programming language!". Such contents can be realized through the following procedures.

 instance=True

 ⬚ while instance:

 ⬚ print("I like This programming language!")

Of course, this program is a dead-loop program. The so-called dead loop means that the loop will not terminate but will continue to run.

This kind of dead loop program is generally not recommended and is only used for demonstration here.

As can be seen, after executing the program, the following contents will be repeatedly shown as an output:

I like This programming language!

I like This programming language!

I like This programming language!

I like This programming language!

    ...

At this point, the reader has learned to write a simple while loop statement without an else clause.

Here is another statement, that explains about while loop using an else clause:

instance=False

⬚while instance:

⬚print("I like this programming language")

else:

print ("This is not a good language")

In this program, because the condition is false, it will enter the else clause to partially execute the corresponding contents, and the output result of the program will be :

This is not a good language

In Python, you can use an if statement under a while statement or you can use a while statement under an if statement. This way of using the current statement or other statements under a certain statement is called nested use.

For example, if you want a program to cycle 10 times, outputting "even" for the first 5 times and "odd" for the last 5 times, you can write as follows:

first=0

⬚while first<10:

if first<5:

⬚print("even")

⬚else:

```
print("odd")
first=first+1
```

At this time, the if statement is below the while statement. The if statement mainly determines whether it is the first 5 outputs or the last 5 outputs, and the variable A is mainly used to control the number of cycles.

The output of the current program is:

even

☐even

even

even

even

☐odd

☐odd

odd

odd

odd

It can be seen that the required functions have been successfully implemented.

In the next section, we will in detail discuss for loop.

Follow along!

⸚OBJ⸛for loop

The for statement in Python is another kind of loop statement and is used very much.

For statements are executed in the following format:

For in collection: execute this section

It can be seen that the for statement in Python is mainly implemented by traversing the elements in the set in turn. The set in question is not a data type of set, but an object composed of multiple elements, which can be a list, a file object, or some other object with multiple elements.

How to use for loop?

If you need to output all the elements in a list, in turn, you can easily use the for loop.

For example, you need to output the following elements of the list

list =["Python", "Java", "Internet ", " Deep learning", "Hadoop"] in sequence, which can be implemented by the following code:

list =["Python","Java","Internet","Deep Learning","Hadoop "]

for instance

list: print (instance)

In this code, the list is defined first, and then each element in the list is iterated through the for statement loop in turn. The instance in the program is equivalent to a variable, and the element taken by the current loop in the list can be obtained every time the variable is iterated.

The instance is just a variable name and can be replaced by other names, such as entity, result, etc.

The results of this program are as follows:

Python Java Internet Deep learning Hadoop

As you can see, each element in the list has been successfully removed in turn.

For statements are often used with the range () function. the range(a,b) function can generate a series of serial data from the number a to the number b, so it can control the number of cycles and the value of i during the cycle.

For example, if you want to output numbers 1 to 20, you can do this by the following procedure:

for extra in range(0,20):

⬜print(extra+1)

In this program, 0 ~ 19 is generated through range(0,20), and the variable extra will be added with 1 each time. Since the value of extra in this cycle is 0 ~ 19 and the data to be output is 1 ~ 20, it is only necessary to directly output extra+1 at the time of output.

It can be seen that the data generated by the range () function are generated in sequence. if the interval between the data to be generated is not 1, but 3, 5, -1 and other numbers, only the step size of the range () needs to be set. In general, the step size is specified in the third parameter of range ().

For example, you can enter the following program:

for example in range(1,10,3):

⬜print(example)

The output at this time is:

1

⬜4

7

It can be seen that the interval between the data is the set step size of 3.

Next, let's look at a for statement with nesting.

For example, if it is necessary to sequentially determine whether each number from 1 to 10 is an even number or an odd number and output the determination result, it can be realized by the following procedure:

For instance in range (1,11):

if instance% 2 = = 0:

print (str (instance)+"even")

else:

print (str (instance)+"odd")

The program judges whether this number can be divisible by 2 through the remainder operation.

If it can be divisible, it means that the number is even, otherwise, it is odd.It can be seen that relevant functions can already be realized by the output shown.

〔OBJ〕 Interrupt Mechanism

In the process of program execution, for example, in the loop structure, when it is desired to satisfy a certain condition or the program is executed to a certain place, the loop or the program is allowed to interrupt execution, that is, the program behind the loop body or the program behind the corresponding program block is not executed, and the corresponding function can be realized by using the interrupt mechanism of program execution.

Generally speaking, the interrupt mechanism is often used in the loop body to better realize the withdrawal and use of the loop.

The interrupt mechanism in the loop body is generally divided into two structures: break statement structure and continue statement structure.

The application situations of these two kinds of interrupt statements are different, which will be introduced separately.

Break statement

The break statement can force the loop execution to stop. A break statement is used in a loop statement. If a break occurs, the execution of the loop will be stopped directly.

The function of a break statement, like its name, is to break the execution of a program. Break statements are often used in loop structures. When a break statement appears in the loop structure, the loop can be forced to stop and then exit the loop.

1. break statement is used in while loop

If a break statement appears in the while loop, it will exit the while loop and continue to execute the following.

For example, if you want to use the while loop to output numbers 1 to 9 in sequence, you can write as follows:

first=1

while first:

⬛print(first)

⬛first=first+1

⬛if first==10:

⬛break

It can be seen that if there is no if statement in the above program, the program will be executed forever and will not stop, i.e. a dead loop will occur. Add an if statement, and then use a break statement in the if statement, which means that if the conditions in the if statement is met, the break statement is executed, and after the break statement is executed, the while loop is exited.

In the above program, A will add 1 to each cycle. When A adds 10 to the value, the output at the top is just 9, that is to say, there is no need to recycle next time and the execution of the cycle can be exited.

2. break statement is used in for loop

In addition to breaking in the while loop, you can also break in the for loop.

In the for loop, you can easily output numbers 5 to 8 using the following statement.

For i in Range (5,9): Print (i)

If you want to output numbers 5 to 7 without changing the above program, you can add the following break statement for interrupt control:

for first in range(5,9):

⯑print(first)

⯑if first>6:

⯑break

In the above program, when i in the loop is executed to 7, the execution of the loop needs to be interrupted after outputting 7, so whether the current I is executed to 7 is judged by if i>6. If this condition is met, I have already reached 7 at this time, and the loop can be interrupted by a break statement.

The final output of the above program is as follows:

5

⯑6

⯑7

continue statement

The continue statement is another interrupt structure statement, whose function is to force the execution of this time in the loop to stop and jump directly to the next execution, which is different from the function of the break statement.

The continue statement is the statement placed in the loop statement to end the loop. First of all, we should know that the loop is divided into many times, and the continue statement terminates the loop, not the loop.

In the same way, let's give you some examples of the application of continue statements.

Here is an example:

```
if(i==22)

print( Enter the statements)

continue:
```

In the above example, the statement will be executed only when the condition is met. If the condition is not met it will continue to proceed with the other statements that are present.

With this, we have completed a brief introduction to loops in this chapter. I hope you had a good time learning different concepts related to Python in this book.

Now it is your time to create your projects and improve your programming abilities.

All the best!

Conclusion

Glad that you have reached the end of this book.

I hope you have enjoyed the content provided in the book as much we loved making this book.

What to do next?

As you have completed a complex and thorough book that deals with Python programming it is now a huge test for you to apply your programming skills on real time projects. There are a lot of open-source projects that are waiting for a contribution. Remember that reading a lot of Python code will also help you understand the programming logics that python possesses.

That's it! Thanks for purchasing this book again and All the best!

www.ingramcontent.com/pod-product-compliance
Lightning Source LLC
LaVergne TN
LVHW051246050326
832903LV00028B/2595

9 7 9 8 6 2 4 1 7 0 0 5 6